Words o
Archang

MW00624540

An Angelical Map for Human Kind

ONE

Journey to a New Way of Being

"It has not been without trial and tribulation that this book has come into being on the border of a new decade, that will reflect great change upon humanity as the time progresses into the new year and beyond. This very moment is a mirror reflection of the future that can and will be influenced by the surfacing of new truths, understandings, decisions, thoughts, and each individual's subsequent actions. Each choice does not only affect the individual having the interaction with self or bearing witness to things occurring outside of the perimeter of your physical instrument and likeness. It affects all things that exist on the level of bio and quantum energetics throughout and beyond what is seen and felt and heard, to the borderlands of accessibility in physical form and the boundless essence of your true form in Light. We have foretold, that this book now held within your hands is an artifact most sacred. It is encoded in Light containing accessible frequencies and information to assist, guide, and transform as you willfully choose. The possibilities are only limited by your own mind and willingness to accept the level of creativity that is available to you."

Archangel Michael

ONE

"The future of human kind rests not on a single individual, nor a group of people willingly led by one who serves as an intermediary to higher consciousness and communication with God. The future of human kind resides on the awakening of the masses to acknowledge and understand that you are an individuation of God. A divine creator of this sometimes delicate yet extraordinarily powerful weaving of a beautiful tapestry called life.

When one is 'searching for something' in life, it's not about 'doing', It is more about 'undoing' those things that have created borders, boundaries and blocks within your life that are keeping you from moving forward, and awakening to the truth of who you are.

In the 'undoing, we go through many small and inordinate deaths, in order to illuminate the truth that is caught up in the web woven of our inner narratives, stories and beliefs that are not aligned with our true path and purpose.

When the paths of deception are eliminated and we become undefinable and liberated from restraint, we fully awaken from our slumber and come to know ourselves as God. A source of knowledge, healing, and illumination with the power to create a new world."

Vox Angelus
"The Voice of the Angels"

Copyright © 2020 by Phyllis G. Douglass.

All rights reserved. Printed in the United States of America.

No part of this book may be reproduced or transmitted in any form or by any means, electronic or mechanical, including photocopying, recording, or by any information storage and retrieval system without written permission of the Author or Publisher, except where permitted by law.

Douglass, Phyllis
ONE - Journey to a New Way of Being
An Angelical Map for Human Kind

ISBN: 978-1-09830-126-2

The purpose of this book is to educate and entertain. The Author of this book does not dispense medical advice or prescribe the use of any technique as a form of treatment for physical, emotional, or medical problems without the advice of a physician, either directly or indirectly. The intent of the Author is only to offer information of a general nature to help you in your quest for emotional, physical and spiritual wellbeing. The Author and Publisher have neither liability or responsibility to any one with respect to any loss or damage caused, or alleged to be caused, directly or indirectly by the information contained in this book and these writings.

www.phyllisdouglass.com

An Angelical Map for Human Kind

ONE

Journey to a New Way of Being

PHYLLIS G. DOUGLASS

FOREWORD

It is a rare event when a gift is brought to humanity by the cosmic intelligence dedicated to its evolution.

Even more rare is the carrier of such gifts. Vox Angelus is such a carrier, and this book is a gift from the cosmic intelligence that guides humanity.

Imagine for a moment what is like inside the human brain, with lightning storms sending information in the form of bioenergy between neural clusters. What we experience as language, matter, and three-dimensional reality, the brain experiences as electrical light storms in a gelatinous medium. Now, imagine a cosmic intelligence where each star is but a neuron. The world, language, and reality that such an intelligence experiences is unfathomable to us - too large in scale for our minds to comprehend.

What Vox Angelus (Phyllis Douglass) has done in this book, however, is to glimpse the synaptic signals within the brain of this cosmic intelligence and downloaded the raw data in symbolic and aural form.

Read this book and you will align your own neural activity to the rhythms and synapses of the cosmic mind.

What does it mean to read this book? Even that, the simple act of reading, requires from us a paradigm shift, because we cannot read this book in the way any other book written in human language can be read. We have to bypass the normal understanding of the conscious brain. We must simply engage each page with our attention, and connect with the symbols visually and through the sounds of Vox Angelus' voice. To look at the symbols and listen to that angelic voice is to attune your nervous system to the higher, cosmic mind. It is that simple, and that profound.

What changes can you expect? Don't. Experience and you will see for yourself in the months and years to come the effect alignment with a cosmic entity has in your world.

Vox Angelus is one of a handful of Aka Dua Level 5 adepts. The work of shamanic art you have in your hands is a testament of this lofty attainment.

Thank you, Vox Angelus, for such an impressive and useful contribution to the Great Work!

Koyote the Blind
Author of *The Golden Flower*

INTRODUCTION

Phyllis Douglass is a very unique individual and has spent many years in keeping her most spiritual gifts hidden until this book! Her vast knowledge of the human condition is now brought forth into the place of Angelic help.

Make sure, to all of you who witness this information, that it assimilates within you in stages. Be mindful, present and thoroughly patient. The awareness brought forth in all of the symbols is somehow going to resonate in different ways for each individual. Phyllis has a very distinct manner of communicating with the Angelic realm. This will provide many levels of guidance to those who may have pondered this connection previously.

For those of you who are new travelers to this information, give time in silence and stillness to assimilate that which is manifested, not only with regards to the symbols but the resonance of the frequency in which they are given! The more often you engage with the transmitted Angelic language, a deeper and more divine awareness will be cultivated within you.

Phyllis has the ability to transcend the typical messages from all our higher wisdom. The Angelic realms have given all of humanity the task of guidance and many of us have learned to ignore this divine connection.

This information is a way for humanity to become, once again, familiar with the clear and constant signals and interventions of the Angels all around us!

One Love.

Caelum Dante Miller

"I am Caelum Dante, a presence in the aspect of our Divine Creator. My purpose is to enhance the enlightenment of all who

travel this Mother Earth now. Measure not the value on your journey, but focus all of your heart to the great love, which we are all a part of!

I am the one for the time now. My direct relationship with our Divine Creator is a result of an accident as a toddler, which was intended to happen. It is an ongoing test of those who are willing to make changes to decide to continue being the God-given best they can truly demonstrate. If I can do it, then anyone who is not compromised can make the choice freely. I only have the limits of choice that prevent me from easily enjoying things that so many others take for granted. This is just the way of my agreement with God."

A HAIKU

In the beginning,
Heavy was my heart and mind
Now free of restraint.

PART ONE

How It Begins

"The journey belongs to the one who is traveling, the Angels say. Not to those who have chosen to walk with you at points throughout the journey."

HOW IT BEGINS

This book flowed through me as an intricate weaving of tendrils of light, containing the vibratory frequencies and sacred symbology inherent to the Angelical Adamic Language of God.

As an Angelic and multidimensional conduit, I am able to understand and translate the encoded frequencies and symbols into spoken and written word, imagery, and art that is understood and assimilated on a soul level.

The creation of each page was an individuated process of birthing something new and unrealized into the world. Each day that my attention was drawn to this magical and sacred artifact, the interaction served as the next rung up a ladder to self-realization on a journey of and for the ascension of the Soul.

It was a voyage through internalized layers of untruths to the sweet remembrance of who and what I Am.

My ability to create this book required complete surrender to the will of God and the ability to detach from everything I thought I knew and believed about myself and the world.

This level of detachment left me feeling empty for a time. Even lonely. There was nothing remaining to latch onto when, for all intents and purposes, my identity was erased. It took time to realize that the identifying markers I'd created throughout my chosen life experiences, such as child, daughter, victim, and friend, were just that—a way to highlight aspects of my life for future remembrance, just like I would a school textbook when studying for an exam. It was required or I needed to remember the answers so I knew who I was, could prove who I was to others, or could hide behind names, titles, preconceived notions and conditioning, to keep me from becoming acquainted with my true nature.

None of our experiences define who we truly are. We are individuations of God having physical experiences from our first in-breath to our final out-breath. I'm a Wife because I chose to marry. A Mother because I chose to have a child. A Writer because I write. A Teacher because I teach, and so forth.

This books completion required a breakthrough in consciousness revealing all that had been hidden or forgotten from within myself.

In conversation with the Angels, they stated earlier on and often reiterate that I must acknowledge and accept that they are intermediaries acting on God's behalf. So when they speak, they are relaying the word of God and no other.

While creating this book, the act of drawing each symbolic image opened an access point or doorway for higher knowledge, healing and transformation. In so doing, this stream of communication with God, the Supreme Being, was wed with the wellspring of inspiration, creativity and idealism existing within humanity, and an Angelical map was born to guide others through the journey needed to understand, reawaken, and remember who they truly are.

The wonders really never cease as I look out upon the landscape of my life. I'm never without surprise and gratitude as to how things play out, even when I'm not doing my best to cooperate with the universe, and stay in the flow of ease and grace.

When I look back at those inopportune moments where the best decisions were not made, I've now taken on the role of a curious and learned witness, versus a victim caught up in the emotional turmoil of juxtaposed circumstances.

As I wrote this book—or more accurately, birthed it—I was taken through a series of tests and initiations. Each image was downloaded in sequential order. I would be gently nudged to sit down and place pen to paper, and when I acquiesced the image would come through and I would effortlessly draw.

As I drew, an electrical current would flow through my body, as the divinely encoded information flowed like water off my fingertips onto the page. At times I would suddenly pause with my pen hovering above the page in a holding pattern. . . Waiting. . . Waiting, and then the pen would once again connect with the paper, revealing another layer. I intuitively knew when an image had been completed.

As I then began to write below each image in my Angelical Adamic Language, the energy emanating from the image was palpable as I transcribed the initiatory prayer. Each page is a separate transmission with a very specific purpose and desired outcome. As the book was completed, I myself voyaged through the process the Angels have set forth for humanity within its pages.

At no point did the logical mind come into play.

Until I had personally experienced the desired outcome of each page's content, the next image in the series would not come. Sometimes I drew two or three in one day, and other times it was several days to a week or so in between when the effects were particularly potent.

At two stages I laid out the pages that had thus far been completed for my spiritual community to preview. I had not realized their powerful essence until I stood agape within its palpable vibratory emanation. I did not fully know what it all meant, but I knew in my heart that this was something very different. All present could feel it.

When the book was almost complete, I felt an urging to look through some of my old journals. I was astounded to come upon references to this book and its beginnings to varying degrees, all the way back to 2007!

Each attempt shared the title "ONE." And each petered out after a few pages, because my logical mind was unwilling to allow the book to write itself.

The Angels waited.

The Angels have always reminded me that simplicity is the key to allowing humanity to arise with relative ease, to a conscious understanding of the depth and meaning of our existence. When we accept our true divine nature, we are capable of powerfully creating our own reality and positively influencing the lives of others.

Our willingness to pay forward acts of kindness and generosity while remaining detached from any outcome of our actions is the caveat that many people consider to be a challenge—and worthy opponent—within the world and culture that presently exists.

It is not easy, but we must learn to trust and have faith in the unseen, the unknown, and the intangible.

We are firstly here for our own experience, but we do not, nor have we ever, operated alone. We are meant to have the companionship and camaraderie of "each other" in states of unconditional love, compassion, respect and appreciation. We are meant to be in relationship with "all things" in gratitude, reciprocity, and awakened awareness. And we are meant to walk this journey hand-in-hand and side-by-side with the God of our understanding, consciously connected and in direct communication in all ways with all things.

My Angelical Adamic Language is as God speaks and the first pure language spoken by Adam within the Garden of Eden. It is the frequency-based language of the soul.

Written in the Angelical Adamic Language and divinely encoded, this book serves as an access point for one's process of ascension and reunification with their own divinity, the "I

Am" presence, the seed of the Supreme Being that lies within the heart of the soul.

The source of our tomorrows lies in setting ourselves free.

PART TWO

The Reason Being

"How far can thy come, the Angels say.
As far as you dream on each given day."

THE REASON BEING

In your hands in this moment, you hold an angelically transmitted and sacred artifact that is a frequency-based alchemical technology, to assist the awakening and ascension of human kind. As a sacred artifact, the Angels stated that this book must never be published in a digital format, as merely being in the presence of the physical book serves as a catalyst for change. This book, *ONE: Journey to a New Way of Being*, emanates divinely encoded frequencies through symbolic imagery and the Angelical Adamic Language of God.

Each of the pages has a focused intent, and the book in its entirety is a spiritual voyage designed to draw the aspirant through a spiritual process, to benefit all levels of one's being.

I was guided to create this alchemical tome in order to assist the elevation of humanity, by sharing the truth of who we are. Most people identify with being human beings, but in reality, the physical vehicle that we inhabit is exactly that. A vehicle.

Our true essence is that of God. An individuation of the creator of all things having a romp upon the planet - a physical experience dressed in a suit of flesh with a beating heart and quizzical mind. And a life is the result of a series of experiences one after the other, until the meat suit is cast aside and we transition into our true form, on the flow of a final exhalation.

The truth of who you are remains untouched no matter what life throws at you.

The time has come. We are destined for bigger and better things, with higher aspirations for our world and our species. Higher aspirations for all things that are experiencing an existence alongside us or within us, differentiated only by rate of vibration corresponding with its form and function.

Throughout our lives we traverse through fields of vibration and swirling patterns of light, that reflect back to us a specific form and function within our reality. We in turn, as a reflection of vibration and light, behold our physical essence within a universe shared, perceived and experienced by all things. What happens to you is happening to everyone through our energetic connectivity.

This book is significantly different from the norm in that it is a magical technology. Though seen and heard like your native and acquired languages, it is recognized on a soul level. Its vibration and meaning bypasses the human mind, and gains access through the heart like a long, forgotten lullaby from childhood, that still serves as a soothing mechanism for the mind and body.

With circumspection and the turn of each page, this book can change the trajectory of your life!

The emanations flowing from each individual page and the book as a whole will begin an alchemical process of spiritual awakening and evolution from this moment forward, no matter where you are starting from.

In using this book, you must be open to change, and allowing the angelical frequencies to begin creating the space and alchemical measure needed to release past beliefs, conditioning, trauma and karmic load that is influencing your future actions. And you must remember and understand that change doesn't take place in a vacuum. True mind-altering change and growth resides within the realm of discomfort.

You will find yourself in a very different place when you've voyaged through the entirety of this book, then when you first felt its beckoning pull and curiosity got the best of you. And each time you accept the opportunity to voyage, you will gain another quantum-level experience and outcome.

The alchemy portion of this book is similar to Tarot, which is said to contain the entirety of the Universe within its four Suites, four Elements and twenty-two Paths. I am not an aspirant of the Tarot, but this has great significance in regards to the formulation of this book.

This book, like the Tarot, serves as a map of the individual consciousness and the consciousness of God.

In essence, *ONE* is an alchemical technology made up of prescriptively encoded and frequency-based formulations, capable of bypassing negative influences, patterns, beliefs and Karmic debt, to manipulate light and vibration, and initiate an evolutionary restructuring of consciousness to align you with your truth and divinity.

HOW TO USE THIS BOOK FOR ALCHEMICAL TRANSFORMATION

There are a few uses that I will share, and many more you will most likely intuitively ascertain, upon your first completion of this book and familiarity with its contents.

Each of the images are multidimensional, and serve as a doorway for the alchemical structure to exist within the physical realm.

This stated, each page is a gateway for higher consciousness and spiritual understanding relative to the vibrational construct, employed frequencies, and meaning of each page. The meaning construed from each page and your interpretation thereof, may differ from one person to the next in any given moment. The vibrational emanation may take on a different context as well based on your level of consciousness, state of mind, the direction of your path, and how you are emotionally and physically functioning.

First, you will need to access and download the free corresponding audiobook recorded with the Angels, "The Angelical Adamic Encoded Readings of *ONE*," at the following link:

www.phyllisdouglass.com/one_audio

You will need to download and save the file onto a computer or laptop. From there it can be synched or shared with another device of your choosing. When listening to the audiobook, I suggest the use of headphones to deepen the acoustical sound experience, though it is not necessary.

The corresponding audiobook itself is not a necessary component, but was added per my request, as the element of sound, which transcends all barriers, allows for a deeper understanding and a truly multidimensional experience with the material.

Whether you are new to an experience such as this or an experienced spiritual voyager, listening to the audio recording as you view each page, helps you to maintain the focus of your attention and guide you through the spiritual transmission process.

I suggest that you listen to this recording as you follow along in the book the first time through. On subsequent passages through the book, you may choose to do otherwise.

PORTAL OPENINGS

The pages marked as a Portal Opening towards the end of this book, may be utilized individually for interdimensional travel and access to magical realms or chambers. Choose the Portal Opening that most resonates with you in the moment, to use with your specific practice such as shamanic journeying. Place your focus and intent as you will, and move through it to the other side.

TO BEGIN THE VOYAGE

Find a place where you can sit without interruption from external distractions. Make sure that you are comfortable and your body is well hydrated, as energy and electrical impulse flow on the inner waters of the body.

Holding the book in your hands, take several deep, cleansing breathes and close your eyes.

State out loud or silently within:

"I begin the ONE journey."

Then take several more, deep breaths in through the nose and out through the mouth.

1) As you breathe in through the nose, follow your breath with your awareness down the *front* of your spine to the tip of your tailbone.
2) As you exhale, reverse the focus of your awareness to follow the breath as it flows up and outward through the mouth.
3) Each time you exhale, use the release to let go of excess tension, and allow yourself to relax even more with each intake and out breath.

When you begin to feel *different*, you are ready to start experiencing the book. You may feel a variety of energetic sensations around and throughout your body as the frequencies of the Angels and the alchemical emanations from the book surround you, creating a pure and sacred chamber in which to do this work.

Listen to the **"The Angelical Adamic Encoded Readings of ONE"** audiobook as it guides you through page by page.

You will note that the essence of *ONE* uses the Roman Numerical System for page numbering. This serves a magical purpose as well.

As you voyage through the book, your own intuition may guide you to pause the recording to linger on an image, before continuing onward. Having travelled through sensitive spaces, the support of the breath is a key mode of transportation through physical, emotional and spiritual terrain. Remember to breathe.

The belief in a higher power is not key, nor is an understanding of what that might look like, because the height of that knowledge and understanding resides within one's self.

This book is an initiatory process and a mode of transportation to the essence of a higher power that resides within.

With each reading of this book, your experience with the material will be different because you are initiating and flowing through a process that continues to elevate the work in progress on all levels of your being – physical, emotional, mental and spiritual.

You are creating space for the infinite light of God to express as and through you in every aspect of your life, as you align with your true path and purpose!

PART THREE

The Essence of One

"This book, ONE, is at the heart of the true essence and expressions of Bhakti Yoga, unlocking one's devotional flame of desire and force of creativity, in order to form a new world within. The outward emanation of that new state of being is what alters the outer world, creating a space for all Beings everywhere to dance within the reflection of their true light and purpose."

The Angels on High

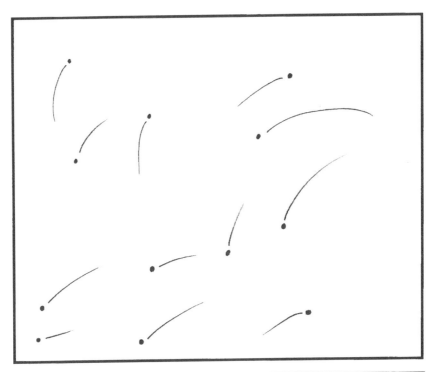

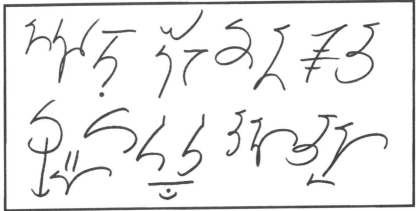

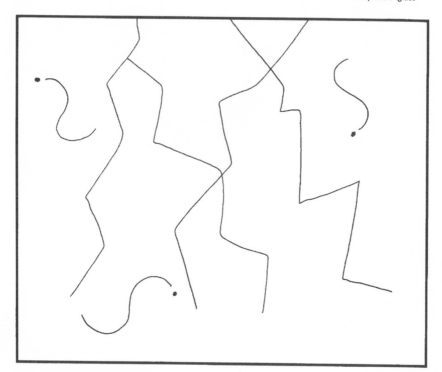

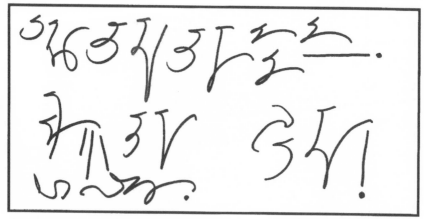

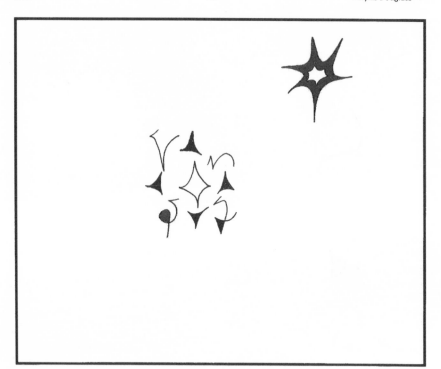

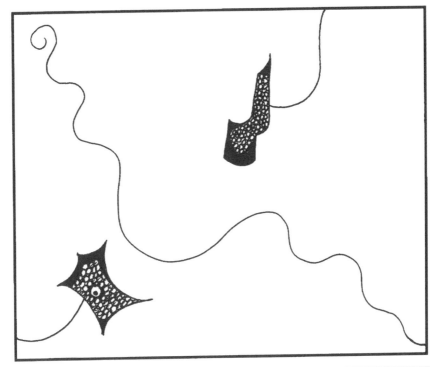

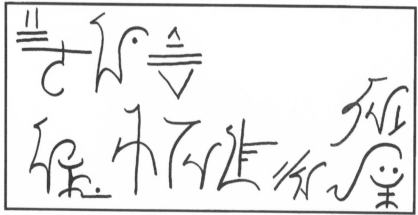

22

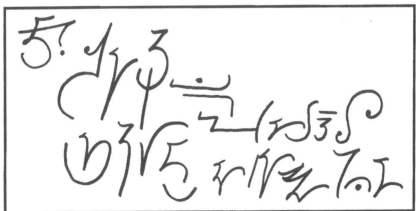

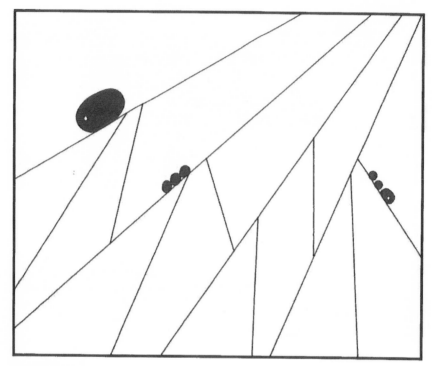

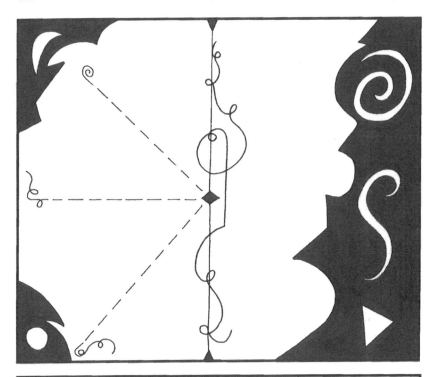

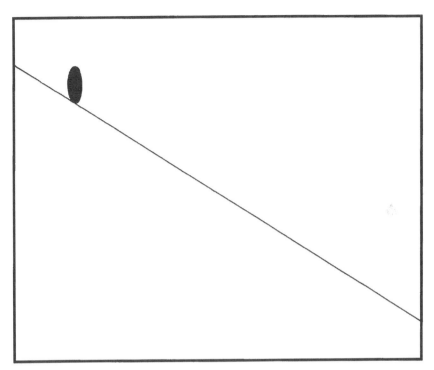

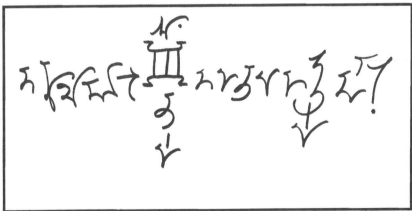

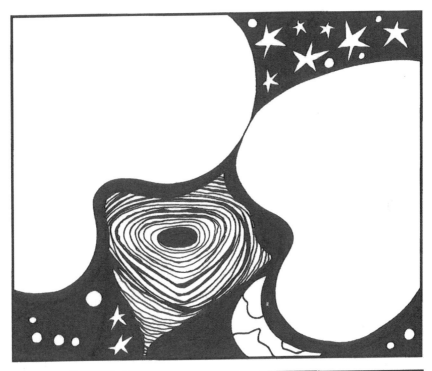

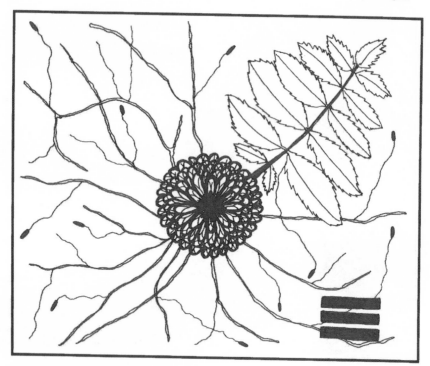

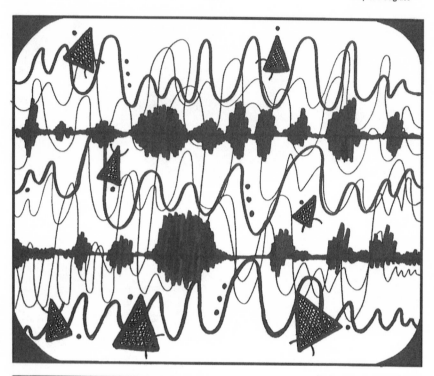

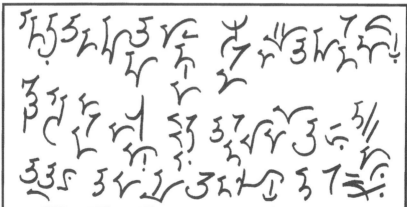

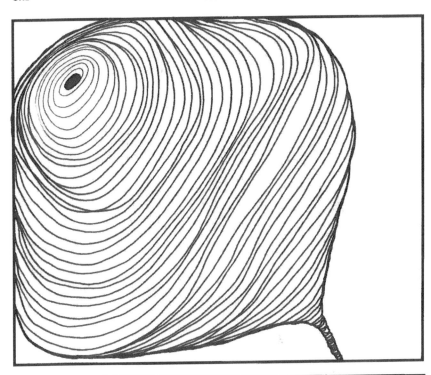

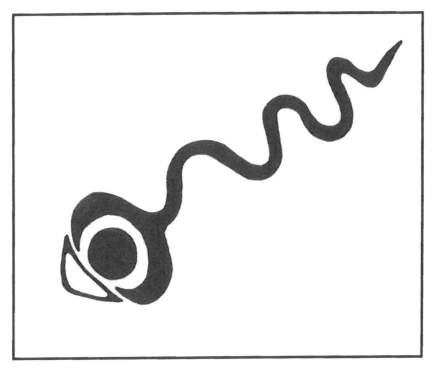

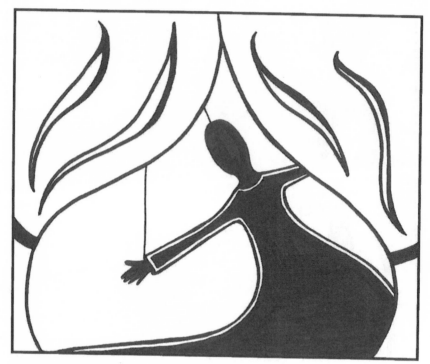

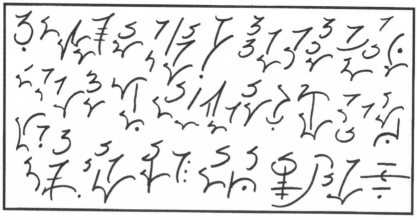

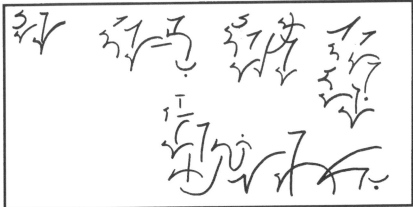

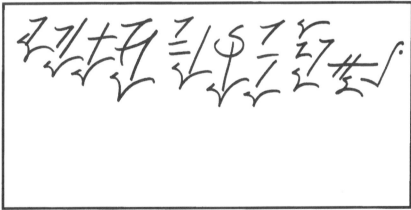

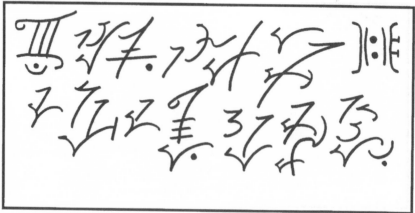

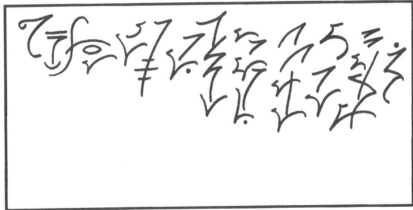

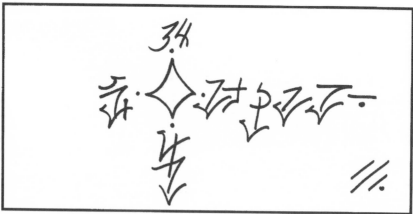

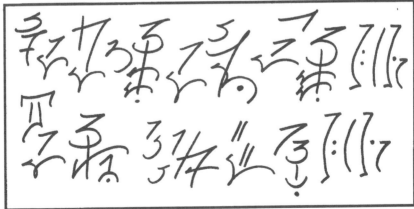

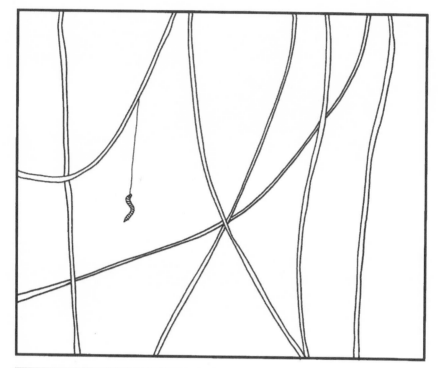

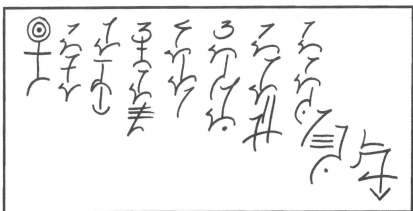

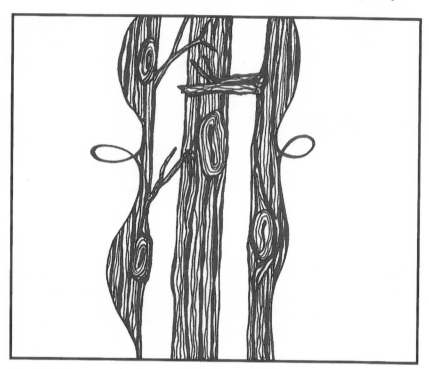

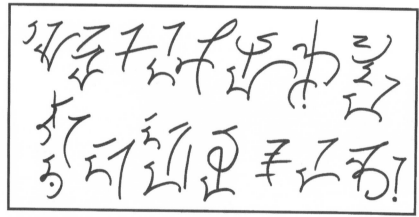

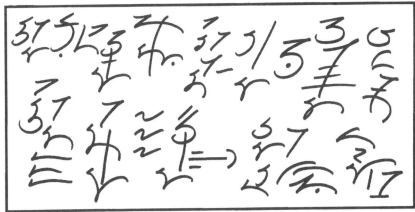

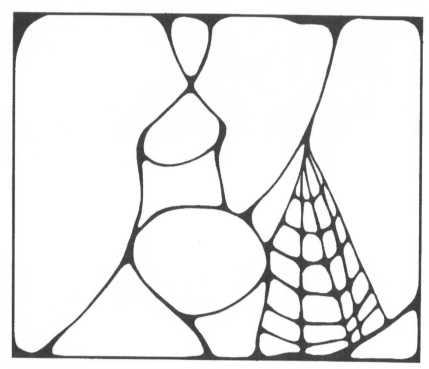

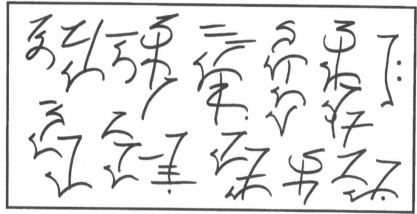

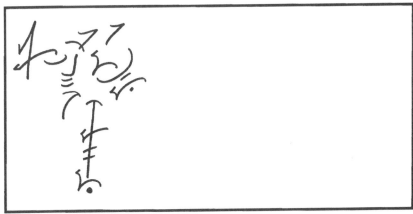

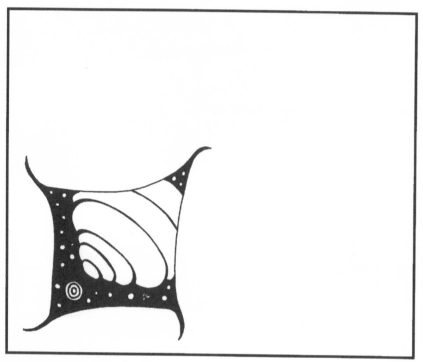

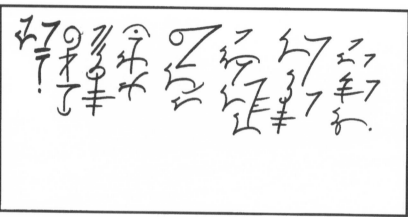

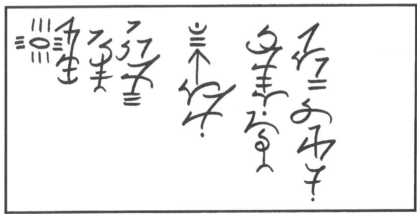

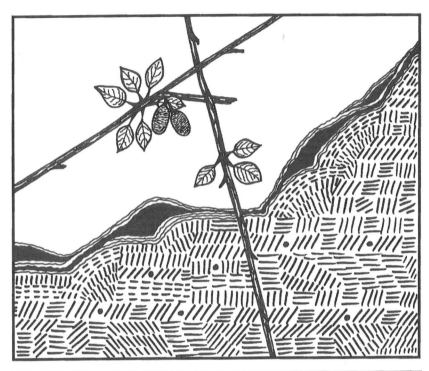

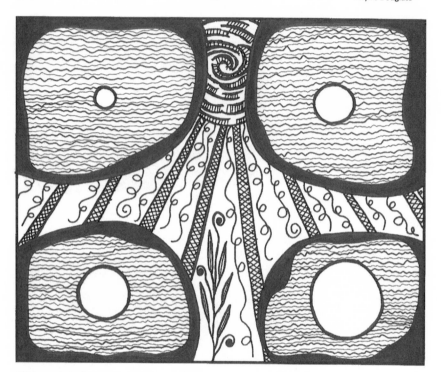

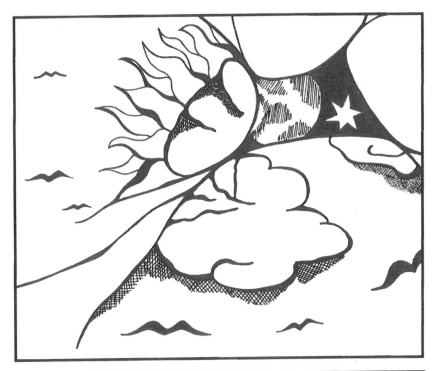

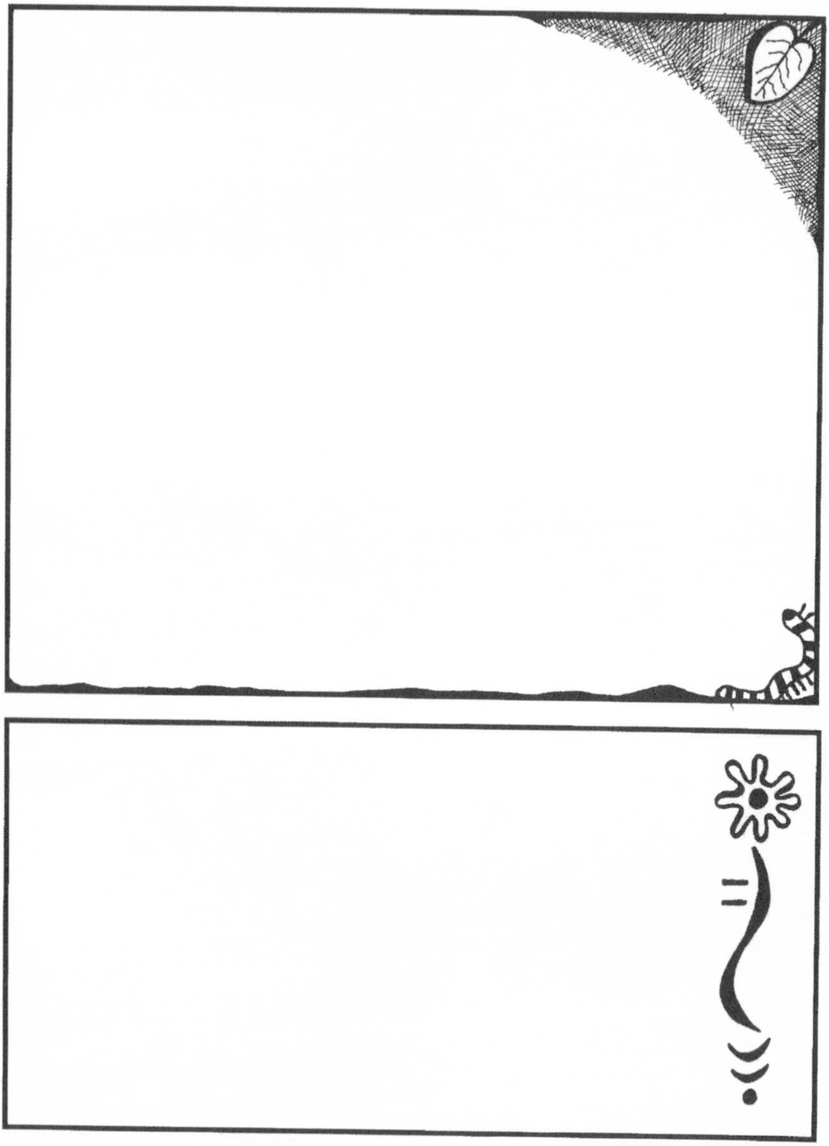

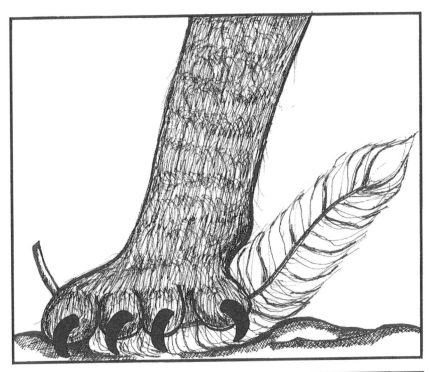

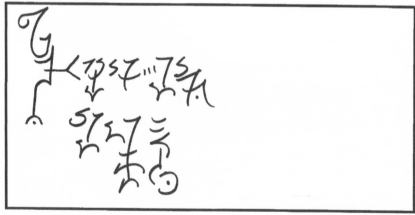

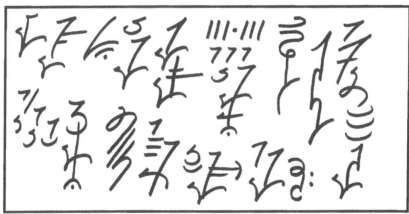

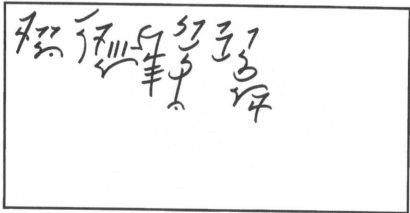

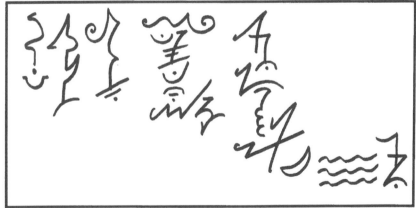

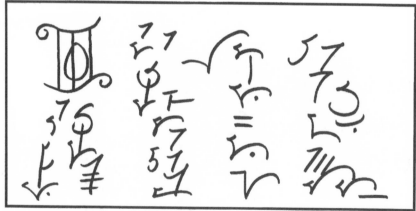

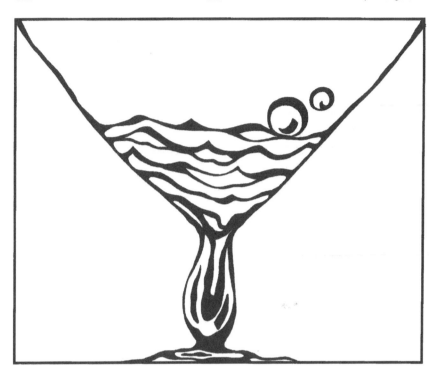

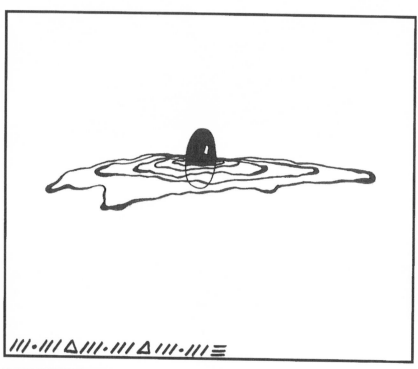

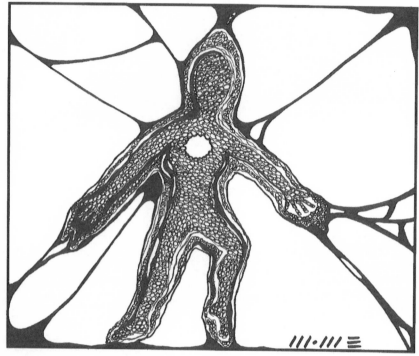

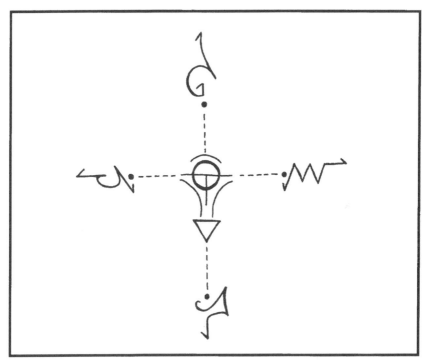

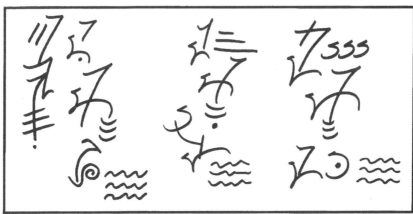

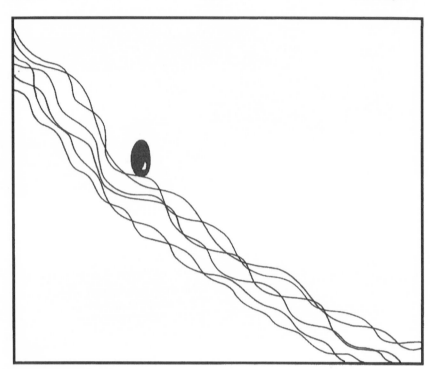

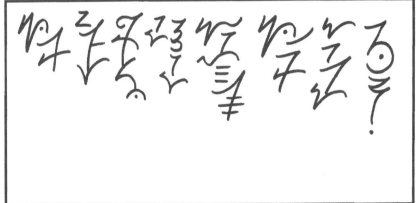

Portal Opening

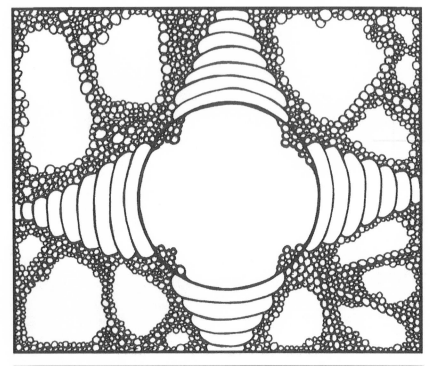

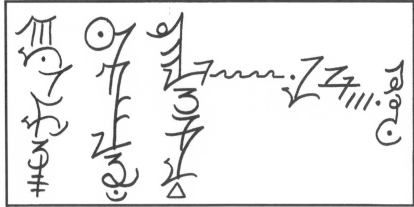

Portal Opening

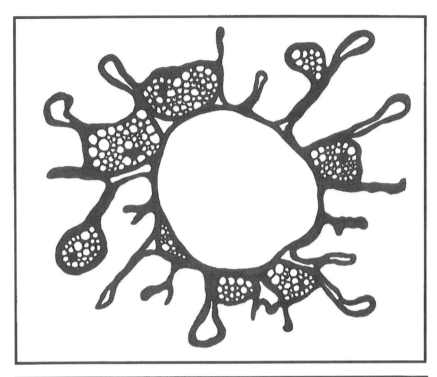

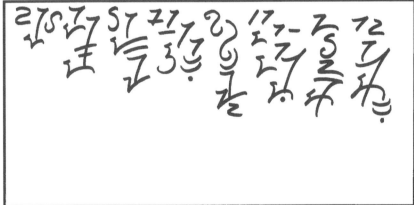

Portal Opening

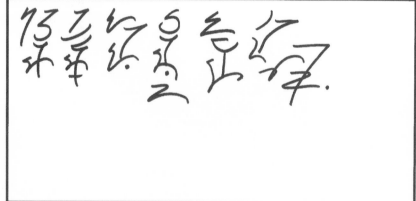

Portal Opening

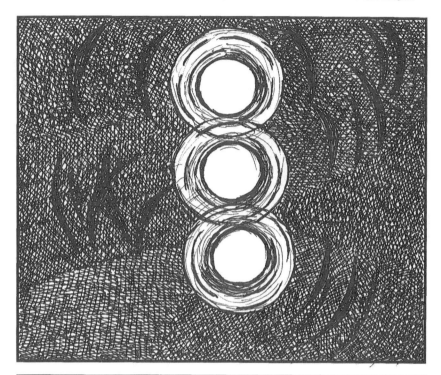

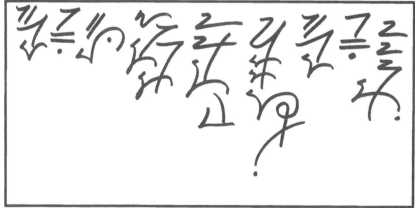

Portal Opening

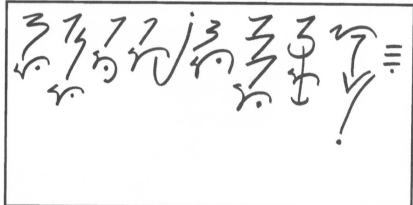

Portal Opening

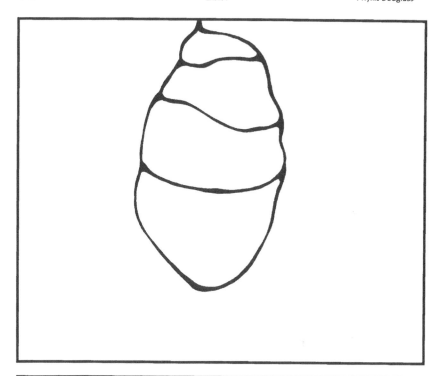

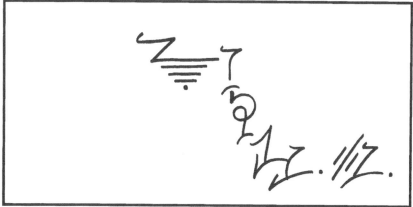

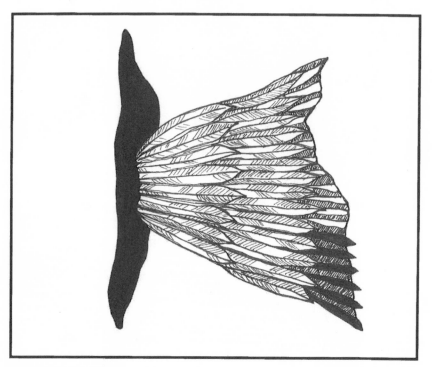

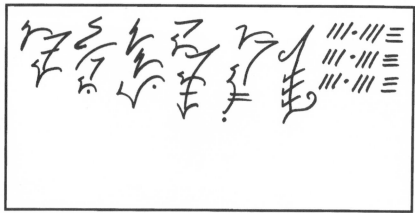

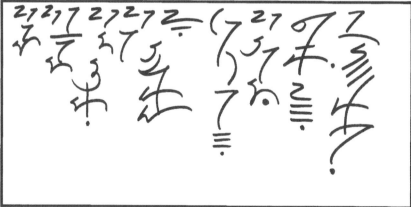

END
TRANSMISSION

Each voyage through is a different experience, and will guide you deeper into new spaces and places from within.

ABOUT THE AUTHOR

Phyllis Douglass is a direct conduit for God, whose spiritual name, *Vox Angelus*, means the "Voice of the Angels".

As an Angelic, she sings and speaks in her Angelical Adamic Language, her vocalizations serving as the carrier wave for quantum light codes and frequencies transmitted as an intelligent force for the healing and spiritual transfiguration of humanity.

When listened to these ancient codes and frequencies are translated and assimilated on a cellular, DNA level, to energetically clear imbalances, trauma, negative patterns, beliefs, and influences; and transmit energetic frequencies, light, and information.

Her path is to share with others the simplicity of communicating directly with God, and how to be spiritually in motion within every aspect of your life.

For information regarding classes, workshops and retreats by Phyllis Douglass, as well as speaking and performance bookings, go to:

www.phyllisdouglass.com

Facebook: www.facebook.com/vocalalchemist